FRESH INSIGHTS

*A Guide to Building Character,
through the Fruit of the Spirit.*

ANDREW V. PUSEY

FRESH INSIGHTS

A Guide to Building Character, through the Fruit of the Spirit.

Copyright ©2025 Andrew V. Pusey
Paper Back: ISBN: 978-1-965593-54-7
Hardcover IBSN: 978-1-965593-55-4

Published by Cornerstone Publishing

A Division of Cornerstone Creativity Group LLC
Info@thecornerstonepublishers.com
www.thecornerstonepublishers.com

Author's Contact

Bishopandrewvp@gmail.com

To book the author to speak at your next event or to order bulk copies of this book, please, use the information below:

6312589729. Cell number
www.andrewpuseyministries.com

Printed in the United States of America.

DEDICATION

I would like to acknowledge the Holy Spirit for the inspiration over the years and the wisdom bestowed upon me to harness resources and write these books. His guidance has been instrumental in influencing lives, bringing transformation, edification, clarification, and encouragement to the body of Christ. The Holy Spirit is the source of our gifts and the grace within us. I am deeply thankful to the Lord for the Holy Spirit.

Key Verse: Matthew 7:20

Wherefore by their fruits you shall know them....

Key Verse : "And now also the axe is laid unto the root of the trees: therefore every tree which bringeth not forth good fruit is hewn down, and cast into the fire."

"I am the vine, ye are the branches: He that abideth in me, and I in him, the same bringeth forth much fruit: for without me ye can do nothing."

CONTENTS

PROFILE

Bishop Andrew V. Pusey was called by God and started with the Gifts at the age of 16. Beginning a lifelong journey of faith and ministry.

He attended the Upper Room Ministries Bible Training Institute, accredited by Oral Roberts University, and graduated in 2003.

While he has also attended other secular schools, he considers Bible School the most important for gaining true knowledge.

Growing in ministry, Bishop Andrew V. Pusey was ordained and attained the esteemed rank of ordained bishop with the Church of God International.

He operates in the Nine Gifts of the Holy Spirit and has a powerful deliverance prophetic & healing ministry, including preaching, teaching, and prophecy.

A firm believer in the five-fold ministry, he is dedicated to equipping and edifying the Body of Christ.

Inspired by the Holy Spirit, he has authored several books, including:

- The Anointing For Possibilities

- The Marriage Mechanic

- Miracle Keys of Real Estate

- The Oil of Etiquette

- Authentic Weapons of War

- Fresh Insights (His current work)

In addition to his ministry, Bishop Pusey is an entrepreneurial real estate broker with over 15 years of experience.

He has successfully completed the Leadership Lab series with the Church of God.

Diverse and versatile in the building gifts that God has given him, he continues to impact lives through both spiritual and professional endeavors.

I am deeply appreciative and thankful for my wife. She is a blessing from the Lord.

INTRODUCTION

A Fruit is produced by sunlight. The fruit goes through 5 stages. First it buds, number two; it blossoms, number three; the green fruit, number four; the full grown fruit and number five;the ripe fruit.

THE TWELVE SPIES SENT TO CANAAN:

- God instructed Moses to send 12 spies (one leader from each tribe of Israel) to explore the land of Canaan (the Promised Land).

- This land had been promised to Abraham and his descendants (Genesis 12:7).

Numbers 13:1-3, 17-20 details the instruction:

"Send thou men, that they may search the land of Canaan, which I give unto the children of Israel…"

JOSHUA AND CALEB AMONG THE SPIES:

- Joshua (originally named Hoshea, later renamed by Moses , Numbers 13:16) represented the tribe of Ephraim.

- Caleb represented the tribe of Judah.

THE DISCOVERY OF THE LAND AND ITS FRUITS:

- The spies explored the land for 40 days.

- They returned with a cluster of grapes so large it had to be carried on a pole between two men (Numbers 13:23).

  » They also brought pomegranates and figs.

  » This demonstrated that the land truly was, as God said, *"a land flowing with milk and honey"* (Numbers 13:27)

THE SPIES' REPORT:

- 10 spies gave a fearful report, saying the land was inhabited by strong people, giants (the descendants of Anak), and that the Israelites could not conquer them.

- This caused fear and rebellion among the people.

"We be not able to go up against the people; for they are stronger than we." Numbers 13:31

JOSHUA AND CALEB'S BOLD FAITH:

- Caleb silenced the people and said:

"Let us go up at once, and possess it; for we are well able to overcome it." Numbers 13:30

- Joshua and Caleb tore their clothes in grief when the people refused to listen and said:

"The land... is an exceeding good land. If the Lord delight in us, then he will bring us into this land..." —Numbers 14:7-8

- They warned the people not to rebel or fear the giants, declaring:

"Their defence is departed from them, and the Lord is with us: fear them not." Numbers 14:9

GOD'S RESPONSE:

- Because of their unbelief, God judged the Israelites, decreeing that:

  » All adults 20 years and older (except Joshua and Caleb) would die in the wilderness and not enter the Promised Land.

  » The nation would wander in the wilderness for 40 years – one year for each day the spies explored the land.

"But my servant Caleb, because he had another spirit with him, and hath followed me fully, him will I bring into the land…" Numbers 14:24

THE REWARD OF FAITH:

- Joshua and Caleb were the only two from their generation allowed to enter the Promised Land.

- In Joshua 14:6–14, at the age of 85, Caleb asked Joshua for the mountain of Hebron, which had giants, and he conquered it, saying:

"…I am as strong this day as I was in the day that Moses sent me…"

SPIRITUAL LESSONS:

- Faith vs. Fear: Joshua and Caleb saw the same giants as the others, but they believed in God's power over their enemies.

- Another Spirit: Caleb had "another spirit" a different attitude of full trust and obedience.

- Delayed but Not Denied: Though they had to wait 40 years, their reward was secured because of their faith.

- Fruit as a Sign: The fruit of the land was a tangible sign of God's promise and abundance.

The Flesh is against the spirit. Galatian 5:19-21

19 *Now the works of the flesh are manifest, which are these; Adultery, fornication, uncleanness, lasciviousness,*

20 *Idolatry, witchcraft, hatred, variance, emulations, wrath, strife, seditions, heresies,*

21 *Envyings, murders, drunkenness, revellings, and such like: of the which I tell you before, as I have also told you in time past, that they which do such things shall not inherit the kingdom of God.*

The fruit of the Spirit will prevail.

Gal 5:22 *But the fruit of the Spirit is love, joy, peace, forbearance, kindness, goodness, faithfulness,* 2 *gentleness and self-control. Against such things there is no law. (NIV)*

Galatians 5:22 But the fruit of the Spirit is love, joy, peace, longsuffering, gentleness, goodness, faith,

23 *Meekness, temperance: against such there is no law. (KJV)*

FRUIT MUST BEAR

According to Matthew Henry Commentary, Jesus cursing the barren fig tree is a symbolic act, a visible parable, not merely about the tree itself, but about spiritual fruitlessness, especially among the Jews and religious leaders of the time.

1. A Representation of Hypocrisy

- The fig tree had leaves, which usually signal that fruit is also present.

- But when Jesus came to it, He found no fruit, only leaves.

- Matthew Henry explains that this is like people who profess religion outwardly (the leaves) but lack true godliness or spiritual fruit (the figs).

"It is the doom of a fruitless professor, to have his profession blasted, and to perish without fruit." — Matthew Henry

2. A Warning to Israel

- The tree symbolizes Israel, especially the temple leaders, who had the appearance of righteousness (religious ceremonies, traditions), but lacked true repentance and faith.

- Jesus had just cleansed the temple, and this act serves as a judgment against the nation's spiritual barrenness.

3. A Lesson in Spiritual Accountability

- Just as the fig tree was judged for having no fruit, so will all people be held accountable for bearing spiritual fruit.

- We are not saved by works, but true faith will produce fruit: love, obedience, repentance, and holiness.

4. An Example of the Power of Faith and Prayer

- After the fig tree withers, Jesus teaches about faith and prayer saying, *"If ye have faith, and doubt not…"* (Matthew 21:21).

- Matthew Henry notes this shows that genuine faith is powerful, but it must be joined with obedience and fruitfulness.

Also, Luke 13:6–9 (KJV):

"He spake also this parable; A certain man had a fig tree planted in his vineyard; and he came and sought fruit thereon, and found none.

Then said he unto the dresser of his vineyard, Behold, these three years I come seeking fruit on this fig tree, and find none: cut it down; why cumbereth it the ground?

And he answering said unto him, Lord, let it alone this year also, till I shall dig about it, and dung it:

And if it bear fruit, well: and if not, then after that thou shalt cut it down."

MATTHEW HENRY'S COMMENTARY ON THIS PASSAGE:

Matthew Henry explains that this parable refers to the unfruitfulness of people who have had many opportunities to repent and produce righteousness, yet remain barren. He writes:

- The fig tree represents the Jewish people (and by extension, all who profess faith but fail to live it).

- The vineyard is the church, where care and cultivation are provided.

- Three years symbolize extended mercy and time for repentance.

- "Cut it down" reflects God's judgment on those who persist in spiritual barrenness.

- Yet the vinedresser's plea shows Christ's intercession, asking for more time and effort to bring about repentance.

The Fruit of the Spirit is vital for reflecting God's character in our lives. It helps us demonstrate love, joy, peace, patience, kindness, goodness, faithfulness, gentleness, and self-control, which truly bring glory to God. These qualities shape our actions and interactions, reflecting His love and truth to those around us.

Having strong character helps us stay true to our values and maintain our integrity in all circumstances.

Chapter One

LOVE

The Greek word for "love" in the Fruit of the Spirit (Galatians 5:22) is ἀγάπη (agape).

Agápē refers to unconditional, sacrificial, divine love, the kind of love that comes from God and is shown through selflessness and commitment. It's different from other Greek words for love, such as:

- Eros – romantic or passionate love

- Philia – brotherly or friendship love

- Storge – familial or natural affection

Agápē is considered the highest form of love and is the foundation of all the other fruits of the Spirit.

One of my greatest experiences of love happened when myself and two other church friends were riding in the

1972 Ford Escort car that ran out of gas on Red Hills Road at 1 Am in the morning . While pushing the car towards the nearest gas station. Across from the KFC ,unexpectedly a young man approached us with a brand new Magnum gun, pointing it directly at us. At that moment, I looked at him and said, "I love you, and God loves you." I believe he saw the light of Jesus in me, which prevented him from harming us. The love of God was truly our protection.

Another time, while walking home from an early morning prayer meeting on the gully banks (trench), a man pointed a gun at me. I looked him in the eyes and said, "I love you, and Jesus loves you." He started trembling and allowed me to pass without harm. The love of God shone through, and I believe he saw Jesus' love in my eyes.

These experiences in Jamaica showed me the profound impact of expressing God's love in the face of fear.

Love is a part of the fruit of the spirit. Love is the main aspect in everything. There are remains three things: Faith, hope and Love but the greatest of these is Love. The word of God says that God is Love. The word says beloved let us Love one another. He that Loves not knows not God for God is Love.

2

There are various aspects of Love:

Love these days is defined as a profound tender, passionate affectionate feeling for another person. They say it is a feeling of warm fuzzy fuzziness. A Feeling of personal attachment or deep affection, passion or desire. They say in the wordly view: It is a strong predilection, enthusiasm or liking for anything.

The Holman dictionary describes love as an unselfish, loyal and benevolent concern for well-being of another. It says the word charity comes from the latin caritas which means dearness, affection or high regard. Today charity is seen as the act of benevolence. Other words for love are devotion to, fidelity, involvment, fondness, piety, regard, respect, appreciation, enchantment, ardor and support.

Love today has become so meaningless my brothers and sisters. Love seems like it is just a ritual or vain repition. Without God in your heart you don't and will never know the meaning of true Love. Love is that pillar which is cragged, grooved and harnest in God. Love is the pure foundation on which every other affection is built.

YOU HAVE SEVERAL FORMS OF LOVE:

- Agape - which is the boundless love of god;

- Storge - which is relationship compassion in marriage and family, we have

- Philia - which is brotherly friendly love philidelphia.

- Eros - which is passionate love which is erotic between a male and a female.

- Ludus - which is flirtatious playful love,

- Pragma - which is commited lasting love.

- Philautia - which is self love. and you can go on and on.

We may have expressed Love in Acts of service towards one another, Physical touch, Quality time, receiving gifts, and words of affirmation. But today I want to talk about a different kind of Love.

Every child of God has the capacity to Love expressively. Love the expressive love. Love is God and God is love; he that loves not knows not God because God is Love. So beloved let's just love one another for God is Love. Love is the oil that soothes the very friction in the engine. It is the the hinges on which every door turns, it is the very itch in your heart that you just can't scratch.

Even for the married ones; you have to learn how to build and strengthen your marriage in every and any way because love is the key. Love is a cornerstone. Love is the structure that keeps you guys together.

I pray that the hand of God will strengthen your love, embolden and give your marriage the courage to be taken to the next level of love, because you'll stand every test of time, and you'll know that the Lord is with you. God bless you. The Lord is keeping your marriage. The Lord is strengthening your marriage. God is the one who starts the good work, and you will perform it on the day of Jesus Christ. So God will strengthen and cause your marriage to be expelled in the right format and the right category because, with God, all things are possible. If you trust and believe and love his holy name.

You can fight a man and he is still your enemy, you can curse him and he is still your enemy, you can utterly destroy him and you have not gained him. If you love him you will win him. Love is stronger than mortality.

The Bible says charity never fails. Love can't fail.

ACCORDING TO PASTOR W.V.GRANT:

"Many churches offer training courses aimed at helping believers develop the fruit of the Spirit. While teaching can provide understanding, the fruit itself cannot be produced through education alone. You can teach about love, but true love the kind that reflects the heart of God can only be received when His Spirit dwells within you.

The Love of God cannot fully enter the heart until carnal, self-centered love is driven out. The "old man" our former nature rooted in sin cannot coexist with the "new man," who is born of the Spirit. These two natures are in constant opposition and cannot be alive in you at the same time.

When the old nature dies, the new nature comes alive. But if the new nature is neglected, the old nature will rise again. Just as the body needs both bread and water to live, the spirit must be sustained through prayer and the Word of God. The Holy Spirit is the living water, and the Word is the bread of life. Failing to nourish the new man will cause him to weaken and fade, allowing the old man to return.

This isn't a different version of you that comes back it's the same old self, with the same tendencies and desires that once held you captive before you were saved. As Scripture warns: *"Love not the world, neither the things that are in the world. If any man love the world, the love of the Father is not in him." (1 John 2:15, KJV)*

A good tree cannot bear corrupt fruit, and a corrupt tree cannot bear good fruit (see Matthew 7:18). The fruit of the Spirit love, joy, peace, patience, kindness, goodness, faithfulness, gentleness, and self-control flows only from a life surrendered to the Spirit of God. It is not learned behavior; it is the evidence of a transformed heart."

The Matthew Henry Commentary has much to say about love, especially Christian love, throughout his commentary. He sees love as central to the Christian life both love for God and love for others. Below is a summary of how Matthew Henry comments on love, drawn from his writings on key Scriptures:

1. Love is the Fulfillment of the Law

Romans 13:10 – *"Love worketh no ill to his neighbour: therefore love is the fulfilling of the law."*

Matthew Henry: *"The heart of Christianity is love. All the duties of the second table of the law are summed up in this word love. If you love your neighbor, you will do him no harm no murder, no theft, no deceit... Love teaches us to value others, to seek their good, and to live peaceably."*

He emphasizes that love is not just emotion, but action and obedience, aligning with God's moral commands.

2. Love Must Be Sincere and Active

1 Corinthians 13 – The *"Love Chapter"*

Matthew Henry: provides deep commentary on this chapter, highlighting that love (charity) is:

- Long-suffering and kind
- Not proud, not selfish, not easily provoked
- Rejoicing in truth, not in iniquity
- The greatest of all virtues

He writes: *"Charity is the brightest ornament of the Christian character. Without it, all gifts, all knowledge, all sacrifice, all faith even to remove mountains is nothing. It is the very soul and essence of true religion."*

Love is greater than miracles, tongues, and prophecy, it is the most enduring evidence of a true believer.

3. **Love Among Brethren Is a Witness to the World**

   John 13:35 – *"By this shall all men know that ye are my disciples, if ye have love one to another."*

   Matthew Henry: *"Brotherly love is the badge of Christ's disciples. It is the distinguishing mark... A fire of divine love kindled in the heart will show in all our actions."*

   He taught that love among Christians is not optional, it is a witness of the gospel to the world.

4. **God's Love Is the Model and Source of Ours**

   1 John 4:8 – *"God is love."*

   Matthew Henry: *"God is not only loving but love itself.*

All love begins in Him. The love He showed in sending Christ is the highest expression of divine grace… Those who are born of God will resemble Him in this essential trait."

True Christian love flows from a heart transformed by God's love, we love because He first loved us.

SCRIPTURE BACKING:

1. **1 Corinthians 13:4-7**

   Charity suffereth long, and is kind; charity envieth not; charity vaunteth not itself, is not puffed up,

   Doth not behave itself unseemly, seeketh not her own, is not easily provoked, thinketh no evil;

   Rejoiceth not in iniquity, but rejoiceth in the truth;

   Beareth all things, believeth all things, hopeth all things, endureth all things.

2. **1 Corinthians 13:13**

   And now abideth faith, hope, charity, these three; but the greatest of these is charity.

3. **John 3:16**

   For God so loved the world, that he gave his only begotten Son, that whosoever believeth in him should not perish, but have everlasting life.

4. **Romans 5:8**

   But God commendeth his love toward us, in that, while we were yet sinners, Christ died for us.

5. **1 John 4:7**

   Beloved, let us love one another: for love is of God; and every one that loveth is born of God, and knoweth God.

6. **1 John 4:8**

   He that loveth not knoweth not God; for God is love.

7. **1 John 4:18**

   There is no fear in love; but perfect love casteth out fear: because fear hath torment. He that feareth is not made perfect in love.

8. **1 John 4:19**

   We love him, because he first loved us.

9. Matthew 22:37-39

Jesus said unto him, Thou shalt love the Lord thy God with all thy heart, and with all thy soul, and with all thy mind.

This is the first and great commandment.

And the second is like unto it, Thou shalt love thy neighbour as thyself.

10. Romans 13:10

Love worketh no ill to his neighbour: therefore love is the fulfilling of the law.

11. Galatians 5:22

But the fruit of the Spirit is love, joy, peace, longsuffering, gentleness, goodness, faith,

12. Ephesians 5:2

And walk in love, as Christ also hath loved us, and hath given himself for us an offering and a sacrifice to God for a sweet smelling savour.

13. Colossians 3:14

And above all these things put on charity, which is the bond of perfectness.

14. 1 Peter 4:8

And above all things have fervent charity among yourselves: for charity shall cover the multitude of sins.

15. Proverbs 10:12

Hatred stirreth up strifes: but love covereth all sins.

16. John 13:34-35

A new commandment I give unto you, That ye love one another; as I have loved you, that ye also love one another.

By this shall all men know that ye are my disciples, if ye have love one to another.

17. Song of Solomon 8:7

Many waters cannot quench love, neither can the floods drown it: if a man would give all the substance of his house for love, it would utterly be contemned.

18. Deuteronomy 6:5

And thou shalt love the Lord thy God with all thine heart, and with all thy soul, and with all thy might.

19. 1 John 3:18

My little children, let us not love in word, neither in tongue; but in deed and in truth.

13

20. Jude 1:21

Keep yourselves in the love of God, looking for the mercy of our Lord Jesus Christ unto eternal life.

THE GOOD SAMARITAN

(Luke 10:25–37)

Lesson on: Loving your neighbor selflessly, even across cultural divides.

Jesus tells of a man beaten by robbers and left for dead. A priest and a Levite pass by without helping, but a Samaritan (despised by Jews at the time) stops, tends the man's wounds, and pays for his care.

Key verse: *"But a certain Samaritan, as he journeyed, came where he was: and when he saw him, he had compassion on him."* (Luke 10:33)

THE PRODIGAL SON

(Luke 15:11–32)

Lesson on: Unconditional, forgiving love of the Father (symbolizing God's love for us).

A son demands his inheritance, wastes it, and returns home in shame. The father runs to him, embraces him, and throws a celebration, showing love and forgiveness despite the son's failure.

Key verse: *"But when he was yet a great way off, his father saw him, and had compassion, and ran, and fell on his neck, and kissed him."* (Luke 15:20)

JESUS WASHING THE DISCIPLES' FEET

(John 13:1–17)

Lesson on: Humble, servant-hearted love.

At the Last Supper, Jesus the Son of God, stoops to wash the feet of His disciples, even Judas who would betray Him. He then tells them to do the same for one another.

Key verse: *"If I then, your Lord and Master, have washed your feet; ye also ought to wash one another's feet."* (John 13:14)

BILLY GRAHAM

(Evangelist)

"When we are filled with the Spirit, the evidence will be seen in our lives. The fruit of the Spirit will begin to grow: love, joy, peace, patience, kindness, goodness, faithfulness, gentleness, and self-control."

Chapter Two

JOY

———∞∞∞∞———

The Greek word for "joy" in the Fruit of the Spirit (Galatians 5:22) is χαρά (chara).

Chara refers to a deep, inner gladness and delight that is not based on circumstances, but comes from a relationship with God. It's closely connected to charis (grace), indicating that true joy is a byproduct of receiving God's grace.

This joy:

- Is rooted in spiritual realities, not emotions or external events

- Often coexists with trials (James 1:2, "Count it all joy…")

Ecclesiastes 5:20 says, "For he will not often consider the days of his life, because God answers him, with the joy of his heart."

I remember seeking the Lord for a life partner, and after much prayer, waiting, and patience, the Lord brought my wife into my life. Our first conversation lasted about five hours, and it was during that time that we truly bonded.

I'll never forget the joy I felt when I first picked her up at the airport in JFK. It was around July 4th time in 2016 and as we met, a special joy and peace filled my heart.

When we got married on October 22, 2018, the joy in my heart was overwhelming. Seeing the bubbling joy in her eyes on our wedding day was a blessing beyond words. As we started our life together, the sense of joy and peace is deep.

The Joy of the Lord is your strength is declared in Nehemiah 8:10. Nehemiah was the King's cupbearer. Anytime you go before a King, you must be happy. Especially when you are the King's butler or baker.

Also in the Word it says; therefore with Joy shall ye draw water out of the wells of salvation.

Joy can be an acronym for Jesus first Others second and Yourself last.

When you put God first, your joy will begin to increase like corn. This joy that Jesus gives, the world cannot give it and the world cannot take it away.

The "Joy of the Lord" as a fruit of the Spirit refers to a deep, abiding gladness that comes from God and is produced in the life of a believer through the Holy Spirit. It is not the same as worldly happiness, which depends on circumstances. Instead, it is rooted in the unchanging truth of who God is, His presence, and His promises.

Galatians 5:22 lists joy as one of the nine fruits of the Spirit:

> *"But the fruit of the Spirit is love, joy, peace, longsuffering, gentleness, goodness, faith..." (KJV)*

Here's how the Joy of the Lord as a fruit of the Spirit functions:

- **Source in God, not in circumstances** – True spiritual joy comes from knowing and trusting God, not from material things or favorable situations. It persists even in trials (James 1:2–3).

- **Sustained by the Holy Spirit** – The Holy Spirit cultivates this joy in us as we grow in our relationship with Christ. It's a supernatural work, not just positive thinking.

- **Strength-giving** – Nehemiah 8:10 says, "The joy of the Lord is your strength." Joy empowers believers to endure hardship, resist temptation, and serve God faithfully.

- **Reflects faith and hope** – Joy flows from our assurance in salvation, our identity in Christ, and the hope of eternal life. Romans 15:13 says, "Now the God of hope fill you with all joy and peace in believing…"

- **Fruit, not a gift** – As a fruit, joy is cultivated over time through walking with the Spirit, unlike gifts which are given instantly.

In essence, the Joy of the Lord is the Holy Spirit's evidence in us that we belong to God, and it reveals itself in a heart that rejoices not in what it sees, but in who it knows, Jesus Christ.

The Commentary Matthew Henry sees joy as a deep, spiritual fruit rooted in a relationship with God, not dependent on circumstances, but flowing from grace, salvation, and fellowship with the Lord. Here's how he comments on joy across key scriptures:

1. Joy Is a Fruit of the Spirit

Galatians 5:22 – *"But the fruit of the Spirit is love, joy, peace..."*

Matthew Henry: *"Joy in the Holy Ghost is a spiritual delight in God and His promises... It is not carnal mirth but a divine gladness springing from faith."*

Joy is evidence of the Holy Spirit's indwelling and reflects inner satisfaction in God, even in trials.

2. Joy in Salvation and Justification

Romans 5:1–2 – *"Being justified by faith, we have peace with God... and rejoice in hope of the glory of God."*

Henry's Commentary: *"The justified believer has cause of continual joy... Rejoicing is a necessary part of the Christian life, for hope in Christ brings a joy the world cannot take."*

Joy comes from knowing we are right with God, not from outward blessings.

3. Joy in Trials and Tribulations

James 1:2 – *"Count it all joy when ye fall into divers temptations."*

Matthew Henry: *"We must not sink under the trials, but rejoice that God counts us worthy to be exercised. Such trials prove and improve our faith."*

Henry teaches that true joy does not fade in adversity, but is strengthened through trust in God's purpose.

4. Joy as Strength

Nehemiah 8:10 – *"The joy of the Lord is your strength."*

Matthew Henry: *"Holy joy will be oil to the wheels of our obedience… The more cheerful we are in God, the more we shall be strengthened to do His will."*

Joy is empowering, not a passive feeling, but an active force that fuels service and perseverance.

5. Joy in God's Word

Jeremiah 15:16 — *"Thy word was unto me the joy and rejoicing of mine heart."*

Henry's View: *"The Word of God received by faith brings joy to the soul. It is the food of the spiritual man, and feeds holy delight."*

Henry highlights the connection between joy and Scripture, as the believer delights in God's truth, joy deepens.

6. Everlasting Joy in Christ

John 15:11 — *"These things have I spoken unto you, that my joy might remain in you, and that your joy might be full."*

Matthew Henry: *"Christ's design is that His joy may be ours, not the fleeting joys of the world, but a settled, satisfying joy rooted in union with Him."*

Real joy is Christ-centered, and it brings fullness, not lack.

SCRIPTURE BACKING:

1. **Nehemiah 8:10**

   "...for the joy of the Lord is your strength."

2. **Psalm 16:11**

   "Thou wilt shew me the path of life: in thy presence is fulness of joy; at thy right hand there are pleasures for evermore."

3. **Psalm 30:5**

   "...weeping may endure for a night, but joy cometh in the morning."

4. **Psalm 126:5**

   "They that sow in tears shall reap in joy."

5. **Isaiah 61:10**

   "I will greatly rejoice in the Lord, my soul shall be joyful in my God..."

6. **John 15:11**

   "These things have I spoken unto you, that my joy might remain in you, and that your joy might be full."

7. **Romans 15:13**

   "Now the God of hope fill you with all joy and peace in believing, that ye may abound in hope, through the power of the Holy Ghost."

8. **Galatians 5:22**

   "But the fruit of the Spirit is love, joy, peace, longsuffering, gentleness, goodness, faith…"

9. **1 Thessalonians 5:16**

   "Rejoice evermore."

10. **James 1:2**

    "My brethren, count it all joy when ye fall into divers temptations…

PAUL AND SILAS IN PRISON (ACTS 16:22–26)

Theme: Joy in Suffering

Paul and Silas were beaten and thrown into a prison in Philippi for preaching the Gospel. Instead of complaining or becoming discouraged, they began to pray and sing praises to God at midnight. Despite bleeding wounds and chains, they were filled with joy because they knew they were in the will of God.

Suddenly, an earthquake shook the prison, doors flew open, and chains were loosed. Their joy became a witness to the jailer, who got saved with his entire household.

Illustration: Joy doesn't depend on your location or condition, it flows from your relationship with Jesus. Even in prison, joy breaks chains.

THE RETURN OF THE PRODIGAL SON (LUKE 15:11–24)

Theme: Joy in Restoration

The younger son wasted his inheritance and hit rock bottom. But when he decided to return home, the father ran to him, embraced him, and threw a celebration. The father's joy was overwhelming, not because of what the son had done, but because of who he was, his beloved child come home.

Illustration: God's joy over one sinner who repents is unmatched. When we return to Him, He doesn't shame us,He rejoices over us with singing (Zephaniah 3:17).

THE EARLY CHURCH REJOICING UNDER PERSECUTION (ACTS 5:40–42)

Theme: Joy in Obedience and Honor

After being threatened and beaten for preaching Jesus, the apostles left the council rejoicing that they were counted worthy to suffer shame for His name. They didn't hide in fear. Instead, they continued daily in the temple and in every house, preaching Jesus Christ.

Illustration: The joy of the Lord gives boldness. When the world tries to silence you, joy gives you the courage to keep standing.

D.L. MOODY

(Evangelist and Preacher)

"The branches of the vine do not toil or struggle; they only bear fruit, and they do this by simply abiding in the vine. So with us: we are to abide in Christ, and the fruit will come."

Chapter 3

PEACE

———∞∞———

The Greek word for "peace" in the Fruit of the Spirit (Galatians 5:22) is εἰρήνη (eirēnē).

Eirēnē means more than just the absence of conflict; it conveys a sense of:

- Wholeness or completeness

- Inner rest and harmony

- Spiritual tranquility rooted in reconciliation with God

I remember migrating to the United States in 1998. Many people advised me against it, cautioning that Christians often got caught up in worldly distractions here. But I felt a profound peace from God and even had a dream that confirmed my decision. It felt like a divine assurance, marking a significant step in my life.

Moving to the U.S. was one of the best decisions I ever made, filled with peace that only God can provide.

I also recall a special moment when I was courting my wife. We were talking by the waters in Babylon late at night, and she shared how she felt an incredible peace in her heart about our relationship.

That peace, which transcends all understandings strengthen your decisions.

It's the Greek equivalent of the Hebrew shalom, which implies well-being in every area, spirit, soul, and body.

Eirēnē is the kind of peace that Jesus refers to in John 14:27: *"Peace I leave with you; my peace I give you. I do not give to you as the world gives."*

There is a peace which passes all understanding. God's peace extends beyond limitations.

According to theologians the peace with God is slightly different from the peace of God.

Peace with God comes through Calvary by justification.

Peace of God comes through the process of sanctification.

It's not a piece of your mind you tell people,

But peace of mind.

We have various kinds of peace:

- **Peace with God** – This is spiritual reconciliation, often described in Christian theology as the peace that comes from being justified by faith (Romans 5:1). It means no longer being at odds with God but being in right relationship with Him.

- **Inner Peace** – Also known as peace of mind, this is a personal sense of calm and well-being, free from anxiety or internal conflict. Philippians 4:7 refers to it as *"the peace of God, which passeth all understanding."*

- **Peace with Others** – This is relational peace, involving harmony, forgiveness, and the absence of conflict with other people. Hebrews 12:14 encourages believers to *"follow peace with all men."*

Peace is the ability to remain calm throughout any difficult storms or situations. Traveling on a cruise across the ocean to Europe or the Caribbean, even though you're on a Cruise Ship. It is not always going to be calm with the waters , but Jesus is still a storm calmer, He is peace in the midst of every circumstance that you are experiencing.

When Jesus was asleep at the hinder part of the ship. There came a storm in the middle of the ocean, in the middle of the night. The disciples said master; do you care that we perish? Immediately Jesus rose up and rebuked the wind and the wave. All Jesus said was peace be still. The Bible says after that there was a great calm.

After your storms there is going to be a calm of peace.

The fruit of righteousness is sown in peace of them that make peace. Peace comes as a seed. Jesus said in Matthew 5 that; Blessed are the peacemakers for they shall be called the children of God.

SCRIPTURE BACKING:

1. John 14:27

Peace I leave with you, my peace I give unto you: not as the world giveth, give I unto you. Let not your heart be troubled, neither let it be afraid.

2. Isaiah 26:3

Thou wilt keep him in perfect peace, whose mind is stayed on thee: because he trusteth in thee.

3. Philippians 4:7

And the peace of God, which passeth all understanding, shall keep your hearts and minds through Christ Jesus.

4. Colossians 3:15

And let the peace of God rule in your hearts, to the which also ye are called in one body; and be ye thankful.

5. Romans 5:1

Therefore being justified by faith, we have peace with God through our Lord Jesus Christ.

6. Psalm 29:11

The Lord will give strength unto his people; the Lord will bless his people with peace.

7. Romans 15:13

Now the God of hope fill you with all joy and peace in believing, that ye may abound in hope, through the power of the Holy Ghost.

8. Hebrews 12:14

Follow peace with all men, and holiness, without which no man shall see the Lord:

9. 2 Thessalonians 3:16

Now the Lord of peace himself give you peace always by all means. The Lord be with you all.

10. Proverbs 16:7

When a man's ways please the Lord, he maketh even his enemies to be at peace with him.

11. Psalm 34:14

Depart from evil, and do good; seek peace, and pursue it.

12. Isaiah 9:6

For unto us a child is born… and his name shall be called… The Prince of Peace.

13. James 3:18

And the fruit of righteousness is sown in peace of them that make peace.

14. Romans 8:6

For to be carnally minded is death; but to be spiritually minded is life and peace.

15. Galatians 5:22

But the fruit of the Spirit is love, joy, peace, longsuffering, gentleness, goodness, faith,

16. Isaiah 54:10

For the mountains shall depart, and the hills be removed; but my kindness shall not depart from thee, neither shall the covenant of my peace be removed, saith the Lord.

17. Psalm 119:165

Great peace have they which love thy law: and nothing shall offend them.

18. Numbers 6:26

The Lord lift up his countenance upon thee, and give thee peace.

19. Isaiah 32:17

And the work of righteousness shall be peace; and the effect of righteousness quietness and assurance for ever.

20. 1 Peter 3:11

Let him eschew evil, and do good; let him seek peace, and ensue it.

JESUS CALMS THE STORM

Scripture: Mark 4:39 — *"And he arose, and rebuked the wind, and said unto the sea, Peace, be still. And the wind ceased, and there was a great calm."*

Illustration: The disciples were terrified as the storm raged around them, but Jesus was asleep, unbothered by the wind and waves. When they cried out to Him, He stood and commanded the storm to be still. Immediately, there was peace.

Lesson: Even in life's most dangerous and chaotic moments, Jesus has power to bring perfect peace. His presence is greater than the storm.

GIDEON BUILDS AN ALTAR TO JEHOVAH SHALOM (THE LORD IS PEACE)

Scripture: Judges 6:24 – "Then Gideon built an altar there unto the Lord, and called it Jehovahshalom…"

Illustration: Gideon was filled with fear, hiding from the Midianites, unsure of his calling. But after a divine encounter with the Angel of the Lord, Gideon received reassurance and peace from God. He built an altar and named it "Jehovah-Shalom" — The Lord is Peace.

Lesson: Peace comes not from our strength, but from the assurance that God is with us. Even when we feel weak and unqualified, His presence brings calm confidence.

DANIEL IN THE LIONS' DEN

Scripture: Daniel 6:22 – *"My God hath sent his angel, and hath shut the lions' mouths…"*

Illustration: Though cast into a den of hungry lions, Daniel experienced supernatural peace. He spent the night in perfect safety, untouched and unafraid, because he trusted in God.

Lesson: True peace is not found in the absence of danger, but in unwavering faith in God's protection and purpose.

Matthew Henry's commentary on peace reveals that it is both a gift from God and a fruit of the Spirit. He treats peace as essential to the believer's relationship with God, others, and within oneself. Here's a breakdown of how Henry interprets peace in Scripture:

PEACE WITH GOD (JUSTIFICATION BY FAITH)

Romans 5:1 – *"Therefore being justified by faith, we have peace with God through our Lord Jesus Christ."*

Matthew Henry: *"Peace with God is the first and principal fruit of justification. It is a settled reconciliation, not a mere truce... We are no longer under wrath, but under grace."*

Peace is not a feeling first, but a position—we are reconciled to God, and this peace is the foundation for all other peace.

PEACE AS A FRUIT OF THE SPIRIT

Galatians 5:22 – *"But the fruit of the Spirit is love, joy, peace…"*

Henry's Commentary: *"True peace is a calm and composed frame of spirit, rooted in faith and submission to the will of God… It keeps the soul quiet in the midst of storms."*

Peace is produced by the Holy Spirit, not by circumstances. It is inner rest, sustained by trust in God's sovereignty.

PEACE AS A GUARD AND GUIDE

Philippians 4:6–7 – *"Be careful for nothing… and the peace of God, which passeth all understanding, shall keep your hearts and minds…"*

Matthew Henry: *"The peace of God is the garrison of the soul, it guards the heart and mind from anxiety, fear, and doubt. It is a heavenly calmness that comes from prayer and thanksgiving."*

Peace is protective, like a soldier standing guard over our minds, when we surrender anxiety to God.

JESUS, THE PRINCE OF PEACE

Isaiah 9:6 – *"His name shall be called... The Prince of Peace."*

Matthew Henry: *"Christ came to reconcile us to God and to one another. He is the fountain of peace, and all true peace comes through Him. Where He reigns, there is peace."*

Christ not only gives peace, He is peace. His rule brings harmony to hearts, homes, and nations.

PEACE WITH OTHERS

Hebrews 12:14 – *"Follow peace with all men..."*

Henry's Commentary: *"We must pursue peace as something precious... It should be our aim not only to be at peace, but to be peaceable."*

Peace is not passive, it must be actively pursued, especially in relationships.

LET PEACE RULE

Colossians 3:15 – *"And let the peace of God rule in your hearts…"*

Henry: *"Let the peace of God have dominion in your life. Let it be the umpire to settle disputes and guide decisions."*

Peace isn't just for comfort, it also acts as a guide. If peace is disturbed, it may be a signal from God to re-evaluate something.

CHARLES SPURGEON

(The Prince of Preachers)

"The fruit of the Spirit is the silent witness to the world of the power of the Gospel. Men may not read our Bibles, but they can read our lives."

Chapter four

LONGSUFFERING
———❦❧❦———

The Greek word for "longsuffering" in the Fruit of the Spirit (Galatians 5:22) is μακροθυμία (makrothymía).

Makrothymía comes from:

- makros – "long"

- thymos – "temper" or "passion"

It literally means "long-tempered" and refers to patient endurance, especially in the face of provocation, difficulty, or delay. It's the ability to:

- Be slow to anger

- Tolerate injustice or offense without retaliation

- Remain steadfast without giving up

This kind of patience is rooted in love and mirrors God's patience with humanity (2 Peter 3:9).

In my late teens and early twenties, I went through a challenging season. I was living in New York, and everything around me seemed bleak. I didn't have many friends, and it felt like I was facing everything alone. My brother was in the military, serving in the Marines, and my cousin was far away in Dominica. It was just me, trying to navigate life in a big city by myself.

At work, I faced additional struggles. The circumstances were tough, and it often felt like I was enduring more than I could bear. But despite the loneliness and challenges, I held on. I learned to press through, relying on my faith with long suffering and inner strength to get me through those hard times.

Longsuffering, if you play with the words, you can get the wordplay suffer long. You have to learn and know how to endure hardship as a good soldier of Jesus Christ.

It takes humility, prayer, and repeated surrender. But the result is Christlike character, refined and strong.

Being longsuffering, which means showing patient endurance in the face of offense, provocation, or hardship.

A transformed mind – Romans 12:2 speaks of renewing the mind. Longsuffering requires that you no longer think like the world, which says "don't tolerate too much" or "cut them off." Instead, you're thinking from heaven's perspective, mercy over judgment.

Spiritual maturity – Children of God grow into longsuffering. It's not just about putting up with people, it's about responding like Christ would, even while being mistreated.

An eternal perspective – When you know your reward is not in this world, you can bear with delays, injustices, or difficult people, trusting that God sees and will vindicate.

A deep reliance on God – It's not natural to bear with others' faults, repeated offenses, or long seasons of waiting without breaking. Longsuffering is a fruit of the Spirit (Galatians 5:22), meaning it must be produced by the Holy Spirit in a willing vessel.

45

A heart grounded in love – Love "suffers long" (1 Corinthians 13:4). You can't endure much from people you don't have love or compassion for.

It was only after Jesus endured the wilderness temptations that He walked in the power to open prison doors and set the oppressed free.

Gethsemane and the cross always precede the power of the resurrection.

Just as fire refines gold, so trials refine the soul. The stars shine brightest against the backdrop of night. Storm clouds give way to rainbows and birth the beauty of blooming flowers.

Consider the lives of Joseph, Moses, David, Peter, and many others, every great victory was preceded by a significant battle.

Even the Captain of our Salvation was made perfect through suffering.

One of my favorite scriptures is Ecclesiastes 11:1 . The Word says cast thy bread upon the waters and though shall find it after many days. This deals with patience. Wait upon the lord.

JOB – SUFFERING WITHOUT CAUSE (BOOK OF JOB)

Job was a righteous man who lost everything,his children, wealth, and health, through no fault of his own. Despite intense suffering, confusion, and harsh words from friends, he refused to curse God.

Key Verse: *"Though He slay me, yet will I trust in Him..."* (Job 13:15)

Lesson: Job endured long seasons of affliction, showing how longsuffering holds on to faith even without understanding. In the end, God restored him.

JESUS – ENDURING THE CROSS (GOSPELS)

Jesus displayed the ultimate longsuffering during His betrayal, unjust trial, and crucifixion. He bore insults, torture, and death, even praying for His enemies:

Key Verse: *"Father, forgive them; for they know not what they do."* (Luke 23:34)

Lesson: Jesus didn't react with anger but with compassion. His longsuffering was redemptive, it gave others a chance to repent.

MOSES – LEADING A COMPLAINING PEOPLE (EXODUS–NUMBERS)

Moses led the Israelites out of slavery, only to deal with constant complaining, rebellion, and doubt for 40 years in the wilderness.

Key Verse: *"And the Lord said to Moses… these ten times have they tempted me, and have not hearkened to my voice."* (Numbers 14:11, paraphrased)

Lesson: Moses interceded for the people many times when God was ready to judge them. His patience and leadership reflect the heart of a longsuffering servant.

SCRIPTURE BACKING:

1. **Galatians 5:22**
    But the fruit of the Spirit is love, joy, peace, longsuffering, gentleness, goodness, faith…

2. **Colossians 1:11**
    Strengthened with all might, according to his glorious power, unto all patience and longsuffering with joyfulness…

3. **Colossians 3:12**

   Put on therefore, as the elect of God, holy and beloved, bowels of mercies, kindness, humbleness of mind, meekness, longsuffering...

4. **2 Timothy 4:2**

   Preach the word; be instant in season, out of season; reprove, rebuke, exhort with all longsuffering and doctrine.

5. **Ephesians 4:2**

   With all lowliness and meekness, with longsuffering, forbearing one another in love...

6. **1 Timothy 1:16**

   Howbeit for this cause I obtained mercy, that in me first Jesus Christ might shew forth all longsuffering, for a pattern to them which should hereafter believe on him to life everlasting.

7. **Romans 2:4**

   Or despisest thou the riches of his goodness and forbearance and longsuffering; not knowing that the goodness of God leadeth thee to repentance?

8. Romans 9:22

What if God, willing to shew his wrath, and to make his power known, endured with much longsuffering the vessels of wrath fitted to destruction...

9. 2 Peter 3:9

The Lord is not slack concerning his promise, as some men count slackness; but is longsuffering to us-ward, not willing that any should perish, but that all should come to repentance.

10. 2 Peter 3:15

And account that the longsuffering of our Lord is salvation; even as our beloved brother Paul also according to the wisdom given unto him hath written unto you...

11. Proverbs 19:11

The discretion of a man deferreth his anger; and it is his glory to pass over a transgression.

12. Exodus 34:6

And the Lord passed by before him, and proclaimed, The Lord, The Lord God, merciful and gracious, longsuffering, and abundant in goodness and truth...

Chapter Five

GENTLENESS

The Greek word for "gentleness" in the Fruit of the Spirit (Galatians 5:22) is χρηστότης (chrēstótēs).

Chrēstótēs means kindness, moral goodness, or integrity. It describes:

- A tender concern for others

- A gracious, upright character

- A disposition to do good and be helpful without expecting anything in return

It's often translated as "kindness" in modern versions, highlighting both inward virtue and outward action. This word reflects the kindness of God that leads to repentance (Romans 2:4).

Watchman Nee was known for his deep spiritual

insight, but also for the gentleness of spirit he carried, even under persecution. He spent the last 20 years of his life in a Chinese prison for his faith, yet those who interacted with him, even guards and fellow prisoners, testified of his calm, gentle, and Christlike demeanor.

I see gentleness as an innate quality within everyone. When you're calm, it's like being a dove, gentle and passive, yet strong in spirit. Gentleness isn't weakness; it's a reflection of Christ's mentality. You're not easily angered or quick to react. Instead, you maintain a calm and peaceful disposition, showing the strength that comes from self-control and understanding. It's a quiet power that reflects God's love and wisdom in our lives.

I remember a time when someone was being sarcastic and disrespectful toward me. I could have gotten upset, but I maintained my posture. I stayed gentle, keeping my character intact. When you're gentle, you hold onto your character because anger can cause you to act out of emotion. Proverbs 15:1 reminds us that "a soft answer turneth away wrath, but grievous words stir up anger." Gentleness is something we must learn to maintain, especially when facing difficult situations in life.

To be gentle is to be more like a dove. You have to learn to be adoptable and sincere in your approach to people. I grew up applying the principle; that a soft answer turns away wrath, but grievous words stir up anger. Whenever you are angry and upset all the time it drains you. Once I was going through a battle twenty add years ago. I remembered Sis Shirley from the Grace Thrillers called me in the midst of the situation and said that: "God sometimes use persons to test the fruit of the spirit in you."

Sometimes your gentleness is tested . The word of God declares that thy gentleness hath made me great. 2 Sam 22:36

An analogies with gentleness are Lamb and Doves.

Lambs in the obvious are:

1. **Gentle** – Lambs are naturally docile and mild-tempered.

2. **Innocent** – Often associated with purity and harmlessness.

3. **Submissive** – They tend to follow and trust their shepherd or caretaker.

4. **Vulnerable** – Physically weak and defenseless, especially when young.

5. **Dependent** – Need constant care, feeding, and protection.

6. **Quiet** – Typically calm and not aggressive or loud.

7. **Clean (Symbolically)** – Represent spiritual cleanliness and sacrifice.

8. **Playful** – Young lambs are energetic and often jump and play.

Jesus was taken as a lamb to the slaughter and as a Sheep before His Shearer yet opened He not his mouth.

Gentleness will make you quiet in the midst of situations.

SCRIPTURE BACKING:

1. **Galatians 5:22-23**

   "But the fruit of the Spirit is love, joy, peace, longsuffering, gentleness, goodness, faith, Meekness, temperance: against such there is no law."

2. **2 Timothy 2:24**

   "And the servant of the Lord must not strive; but be gentle unto all men, apt to teach, patient..."

3. **Titus 3:2**

   "To speak evil of no man, to be no brawlers, but gentle, shewing all meekness unto all men."

4. **1 Thessalonians 2:7**

   "But we were gentle among you, even as a nurse cherisheth her children..."

5. **James 3:17**

   "But the wisdom that is from above is first pure, then peaceable, gentle, and easy to be intreated, full of mercy and good fruits, without partiality, and without hypocrisy."

6. **Proverbs 15:1**

   A soft answer turneth away wrath: but grievous words stir up anger.

7. **Isaiah 40:11**

   He shall feed his flock like a shepherd: he shall gather the lambs with his arm, and carry them in his bosom, and shall gently lead those that are with young.

8. **Philippians 4:5**

   Let your moderation be known unto all men. The Lord is at hand.

   (Moderation here also implies gentleness or forbearance.)

9. **Ephesians 4:1-2**

   ...with all lowliness and meekness, with longsuffering, forbearing one another in love...

10. **Colossians 3:12**

    Put on therefore, as the elect of God, holy and beloved, bowels of mercies, kindness, humbleness of mind, meekness, longsuffering...

11. **Matthew 11:29**

    Take my yoke upon you, and learn of me; for I am meek and lowly in heart: and ye shall find rest unto your souls.

12. **2 Corinthians 10:1**

    Now I Paul myself beseech you by the meekness and gentleness of Christ...

13. Psalm 18:35

Thou hast also given me the shield of thy salvation: and thy right hand hath holden me up, and thy gentleness hath made me great.

14. 1 Peter 3:4

...even the ornament of a meek and quiet spirit, which is in the sight of God of great price.

15. 1 Peter 3:15

...and be ready always to give an answer to every man that asketh you a reason of the hope that is in you with meekness and fear...

16. Romans 12:10

Be kindly affectioned one to another with brotherly love; in honour preferring one another...

17. Romans 14:19

Let us therefore follow after the things which make for peace, and things wherewith one may edify another.

18. Romans 15:1

We then that are strong ought to bear the infirmities of the weak, and not to please ourselves.

19. 1 Corinthians 13:4-5

Charity suffereth long, and is kind; charity envieth not... seeketh not her own, is not easily provoked...

20. Proverbs 25:15

By long forbearing is a prince persuaded, and a soft tongue breaketh the bone.

21. Ecclesiastes 10:4

If the spirit of the ruler rise up against thee, leave not thy place; for yielding pacifieth great offences.

22. Isaiah 42:3

A bruised reed shall he not break, and the smoking flax shall he not quench...

23. Zechariah 9:9

...behold, thy King cometh unto thee: he is just, and having salvation; lowly, and riding upon an ass...

24. Job 15:11

Are the consolations of God small with thee? is there any secret thing with thee? (Implies God's words are often consoling and gentle.)

25. Luke 6:35

But love ye your enemies, and do good… and ye shall be the children of the Highest: for he is kind unto the unthankful and to the evil.

A.W. TOZER

(Author and Pastor)

"A Pharisee is hard on others and easy on himself, but a spiritual man is easy on others and hard on himself. The fruit of the Spirit is a manifestation of that transformed inner life."

Chapter Six

GOODNESS

The Greek word for "goodness" in the Fruit of the Spirit (Galatians 5:22) is ἀγαθωσύνη (agathōsýnē).

Agathōsýnē refers to active moral excellence, goodness in action. It is:

- Uprightness of heart and life

- A deliberate pursuit of doing what is right

- Often expressed in generosity, justice, and holiness

Unlike chrēstótēs (kindness), which leans toward a gentle spirit, agathōsýnē includes a zeal for truth and righteousness, sometimes even correcting or confronting in love (as seen in Jesus' cleansing of the temple).

There was a particular situation where someone was very brutal toward me with their words, trying to pass judgment on me. Despite this, I maintained goodness because I know that being good is a core part of who I am. God is good, and His goodness is a part of me. No matter what others say or do, I hold on to that goodness. It's not something I can lose, because it's grounded in who God is.

Interestingly, the person who tried to bring judgment upon me ended up being incarcerated because of the situation. It was a reminder that, even when we choose to remain good and hold our peace, God's justice still prevails. Through it all, I maintained my character, knowing that goodness and integrity are things I must uphold, no matter the circumstances. Right now In New York, that person respects to the very ground I walk on.

The common phrase states God is good all the time. We have to practice being good in spite of how we are treated. Good is having a lot of sufficiency in us, irrespective of what contrary wind that blows. You have to remain steadfastly good evening in the midst of unfair opposition and oppinion against you.

You can never be too good. Goodness is something that's vested deeply in the believers life by the Holy Spirit.

> *Therefore if thine enemy hunger, feed him; if he thirst, give him drink: for in so doing thou shalt heap coals of fire on his head."* — Romans 12:20 (KJV)

This verse teaches grace under pressure and the power of responding to hostility with kindness. In the context of rage:

- Instead of reacting with anger when someone provokes you, respond with goodness and kindness.

- It reminds you that retaliation isn't your role, showing mercy disarms the situation and leaves judgment to God.

- By choosing peace over revenge, you're "heaping coals of fire" a metaphor for convicting the other person through your unexpected kindness.

This aligns with the broader message in Romans 12:17–21: "Be not overcome of evil, but overcome evil with good."

There are stories in the Bible about goodness:

THE GOOD SAMARITAN

Scripture: Luke 10:25–37

Virtue: Compassion beyond boundaries

A Samaritan helps a wounded man after others (a priest and a Levite) pass him by. This story highlights that true neighborly love transcends race, religion, or status.

THE GOOD SHEPHERD (JESUS)

Scripture: John 10:11–18

Virtue: Sacrificial love and care

Jesus describes Himself as the Good Shepherd who lays down His life for the sheep, contrasting hired hands who abandon the flock in danger.

JOSEPH'S INTEGRITY IN EGYPT

Scripture: Genesis 39–50

Virtue: Faithfulness and forgiveness

Despite betrayal, slavery, and prison, Joseph remained faithful to God and ultimately forgave his brothers, saving a nation in famine.

RUTH'S LOYALTY AND KINDNESS

Scripture: Book of Ruth

Virtue: Loyalty and selfless love

Ruth remains faithful to her mother-in-law Naomi and is later rewarded by God through her marriage to Boaz, becoming part of Jesus' lineage.

DAVID SPARES SAUL

Scripture: 1 Samuel 24

Virtue: Mercy and restraint

Even though Saul sought to kill him, David refuses to harm God's anointed, choosing honor over vengeance.

THE PRODIGAL SON'S FATHER

Scripture: Luke 15:11–32

Virtue: Forgiveness and restoration

A father welcomes his wayward son with open arms, symbolizing God's goodness and mercy toward repentant sinners.

THE WIDOW OF ZAREPHATH

Scripture: 1 Kings 17:8–16

Virtue: Generosity in scarcity

A poor widow shares her last meal with the prophet Elijah, and God miraculously sustains her household through famine.

THE SHUNAMMITE WOMAN'S HOSPITALITY

Scripture: 2 Kings 4:8–37

Virtue: Generosity and faith

A wealthy woman provides room and care for the

prophet Elisha. Her kindness is later rewarded when God miraculously gives her a son—and then restores him to life after death.

THE CENTURION'S GREAT FAITH

Scripture: Matthew 8:5–13

Virtue: Humility and faith

A Roman centurion asks Jesus to heal his servant, saying He need only speak the word. Jesus praises his extraordinary faith, saying He hadn't found such faith in all Israel.

THE WOMAN WHO ANOINTED JESUS

Scripture: Luke 7:36–50

Virtue: Love, repentance, and devotion

A sinful woman weeps at Jesus' feet, washing them with her tears and anointing them with expensive perfume. Jesus forgives her, acknowledging that her deep love flowed from her gratitude.

SCRIPTURE BACKING:

1. Galatians 5:22

"But the fruit of the Spirit is love, joy, peace, longsuffering, gentleness, goodness, faith,"

2. Romans 15:14

"And I myself also am persuaded of you, my brethren, that ye also are full of goodness, filled with all knowledge, able also to admonish one another."

3. Psalm 23:6

"Surely goodness and mercy shall follow me all the days of my life: and I will dwell in the house of the Lord for ever."

4. Psalm 31:19

"Oh how great is thy goodness, which thou hast laid up for them that fear thee; which thou hast wrought for them that trust in thee before the sons of men!"

5. Psalm 107:9

"For he satisfieth the longing soul, and filleth the hungry soul with goodness."

6. **Exodus 33:19**

   "And he said, I will make all my goodness pass before thee, and I will proclaim the name of the Lord before thee..."

7. **Nahum 1:7**

   "The Lord is good, a strong hold in the day of trouble; and he knoweth them that trust in him."

8. **Romans 2:4**

   "Or despisest thou the riches of his goodness and forbearance and longsuffering; not knowing that the goodness of God leadeth thee to repentance?"

9. **Titus 3:4–5**

   "But after that the kindness and love of God our Saviour toward man appeared, not by works of righteousness which we have done..."

10. **2 Thessalonians 1:11**

    "Wherefore also we pray always for you... and fulfil all the good pleasure of his goodness, and the work of faith with power:"

11. **Psalm 34:8**

    "O taste and see that the Lord is good: blessed is the man that trusteth in him."

12. Psalm 145:9

"The Lord is good to all: and his tender mercies are over all his works."

13. Ephesians 5:9

"(For the fruit of the Spirit is in all goodness and righteousness and truth;)"

14. Micah 6:8

"He hath shewed thee, O man, what is good; and what doth the Lord require of thee, but to do justly, and to love mercy…"

15. Hebrews 13:16

"But to do good and to communicate forget not: for with such sacrifices God is well pleased."

JOHN STOTT

(Anglican Theologian)

"The fruit of the Spirit is the natural product of the Spirit's presence and activity within us. It is not manufactured; it grows."

Chapter Seven

FAITH

———⟨✦⟩———

The Greek word for "faith" in the Fruit of the Spirit (Galatians 5:22) is πίστις (pístis).

Pístis means faith, trust, or belief, particularly in a relational sense, implying:

- Firm conviction and reliance on God

- Trust in His promises and truth

- Faithfulness in one's commitment to God

I want to share a powerful testimony of God's provision in my life. When God called me to go to Israel with Pastor Benny Hinn and the team, I knew I had to step out in faith, even though the trip cost about $4,000. I sacrificed everything to make it happen.

The day before the trip, I realized I still needed a certain amount of money to cover my budget. As I lay down on my couch, I reached between the cushions and felt something unusual. I pulled out an envelope with my name on it. Inside, to my astonishment, was a check for a few thousand dollars, an amount that perfectly covered my needs. And the most amazing part? The check's expiration date was that very day!

I rushed to the bank just in time, managing to cash the check before they closed. It was a miraculous provision, a true testament to God's faithfulness. I had no prior knowledge of that check, and it felt like a divine surprise.

This experience strengthened my faith in God's provision and timing. When you trust God with unwavering faith, you will witness His miracles in your life. To God be the glory!

It is more than intellectual assent; it's a living faith that is active, obedient, and relational. It's the same word used to describe the faith by which believers are saved (Ephesians 2:8) and is foundational to a life that pleases God (Hebrews 11:6).

Jesus said in the New Testament. When the Son of Man comes: shall He find faith on earth. Faith is like a key to anything. It's a key to God's storehouse of blessings.

Many cars have keyless entry today. Faith gives us access into the manifold wisdom and blessings of God.

Without Faith it is impossible to please God. The eyes of faith sees the good in every situation beyond our wildest imagination.

As children of God we know that Faith comes by hearing and hearing, by the Word of God.

When we hear God's Word our Faith begins to grow and develop through His infinite Grace.

Faith is something everyone should have. We walk by Faith and not by sight. Our Faith in God, must grow daily. Many believers are stunt in their Faith. Faith can become a dwarf, if it is not fed with God's Word on a frequent basis.

Faith is something we practice. We have some hills to climb, we have some valleys to cross over, we some waters to sail through. We need the Faith of God to endure it all.

When Peter saw the Master of Faith walking on water unaware. The Bible said; Peter had eyes of Faith to ask Jesus if he can also defy gravity. Jesus said come. What I respect about Peter is; that he got out of the boat.Sometimes in order for our Faith to become active, we in turn have to step out of our comfort zones.

Peter began to walk on water. The moment Peter took his eyes off Jesus, he began to sink. But Jesus immediately reached out His hand and held Peter. Sometimes when our Faith begins to waver Jesus stretches His Faith towards us. God will not allow you to fail. Your enemies will never prove their doubts, no matter what the situations look like.

In the believers walk of victory, the believers are to have some level of Faith, depending on God for a victorious outcome.

Faith is greater than fate. Jesus was very pragmatic and practical in His approach to Faith. Whenever we are born again, we are given a measure of Faith, so that we can maximize our benefit of Salvation.

Pastor WV Grant says Faith is like a muscle that needs practice.

We know reference in God's Word about Faith.

THE CENTURION'S FAITH

Scripture: Matthew 8:5–13

A Roman centurion asked Jesus to heal his servant, saying He only needed to "speak the word." Jesus marveled at his faith and said, "I have not found so great faith, no, not in Israel."

THE WOMAN WITH THE ISSUE OF BLOOD

Scripture: Mark 5:25–34

A woman suffering for 12 years believed she would be healed if she could just touch Jesus' garment. Jesus told her, "Daughter, thy faith hath made thee whole."

ABRAHAM OFFERING ISAAC

Scripture: Genesis 22:1–18

Abraham showed great faith when he was willing to sacrifice Isaac, trusting that God could raise him from the dead if necessary. His obedience became a model of faith.

THE CANAANITE WOMAN'S PERSISTENCE

Scripture: Matthew 15:21–28

A Gentile woman begged Jesus to heal her daughter. Despite initial rejection, she humbly persisted, and Jesus said, *"O woman, great is thy faith."*

NOAH BUILDS THE ARK

Scripture: Genesis 6–9

Noah believed God's warning about a flood, though rain had never fallen. He built the ark in obedience, becoming *"heir of the righteousness which is by faith"* (Hebrews 11:7).

THE FOUR FRIENDS LOWERING THE PARALYZED MAN

Scripture: Mark 2:1–12

Four friends carried a paralyzed man to Jesus and lowered him through a roof. Jesus, "seeing their faith," healed the man both spiritually and physically.

THE FAITH OF SHADRACH, MESHACH, AND ABEDNEGO

Scripture: Daniel 3:1–30

These three Hebrews refused to bow to a golden image, trusting God would deliver them from the fiery furnace. Their unwavering faith led to a miraculous rescue and a powerful witness.

SCRIPTURE BACKING:

1. **Romans 10:17**
   "So then faith cometh by hearing, and hearing by the word of God."

2. **Hebrews 11:6**
   "But without faith it is impossible to please him…"

3. **Mark 11:22–23**

   "…Have faith in God. For verily I say unto you, That whosoever shall say unto this mountain… shall not doubt in his heart…"

4. **James 2:17**

   "Even so faith, if it hath not works, is dead, being alone."

5. **2 Corinthians 5:7**

   "For we walk by faith, not by sight."

6. **Matthew 17:20**

   "…If ye have faith as a grain of mustard seed… nothing shall be impossible unto you."

7. **Galatians 2:20**

   "…the life which I now live in the flesh I live by the faith of the Son of God…"

8. **Hebrews 11:1**

   "Now faith is the substance of things hoped for, the evidence of things not seen."

9. **Luke 17:5**

   "And the apostles said unto the Lord, Increase our faith."

10. Jude 1:20

"But ye, beloved, building up yourselves on your most holy faith, praying in the Holy Ghost."

11. 1 Timothy 6:12

"Fight the good fight of faith, lay hold on eternal life..."

12. Romans 1:17

"...The just shall live by faith."

13. Ephesians 6:16

"Above all, taking the shield of faith, wherewith ye shall be able to quench all the fiery darts of the wicked."

14. Philippians 1:6

"...he which hath begun a good work in you will perform it until the day of Jesus Christ:"

15. Colossians 2:6–7

"As ye have therefore received Christ Jesus the Lord, so walk ye in him: Rooted and built up in him, and stablished in the faith..."

16. 2 Thessalonians 1:3

"...your faith groweth exceedingly, and the charity of every one of you all toward each other aboundeth;"

17. 1 Peter 1:7

"...the trial of your faith, being much more precious than of gold..."

18. James 1:3–4

"Knowing this, that the trying of your faith worketh patience..."

19. Romans 5:1–2

"...we have access by faith into this grace wherein we stand..."

20. 1 John 5:4

"...this is the victory that overcometh the world, even our faith."

21. 2 Peter 1:5–7

"...add to your faith virtue; and to virtue knowledge..."

22. Psalm 37:5

"Commit thy way unto the Lord; trust also in him; and he shall bring it to pass."

23. Proverbs 3:5–6

"Trust in the Lord with all thine heart; and lean not unto thine own understanding..."

24. Matthew 21:22

"And all things, whatsoever ye shall ask in prayer, believing, ye shall receive."

25. 1 Thessalonians 5:24

"Faithful is he that calleth you, who also will do it."

ANDREW MURRAY

(South African Theologian)

"The fruit of the Spirit is the outward expression of Christ dwelling in the heart by faith."

Chapter Eight

MEEKNESS
———⟨⟨⟩⟩———

The Greek word for "meekness" in the Fruit of the Spirit (Galatians 5:22) is πραΰτης (prautēs).

Prautēs means gentleness or humility and refers to:

- A controlled strength or strength under control, not weakness

- A humble and teachable attitude

- A gentle, submissive spirit that does not seek to retaliate but is patient and kind, even in adversity

In 2015 I went to Guyana on a mission trip. At the end of the trip: Bishop Andrew Binda and his wife looked at me and said, "Andrew, you are a nice person, in other words, a meek humble person, but you're not a pushover." They understood that meekness means being humble, but it doesn't mean being weak or allowing others to walk over you. You can be humble and still stand firm, knowing when to show strength without compromising your character.

It reflects the attitude Jesus demonstrated in Matthew 11:29, where He describes Himself as "gentle and humble in heart," and is often associated with a servant's heart and a willingness to yield to God's will.

meekness is never weakness Meekness actually is strength from God Himself. You don't need to prove anything to anyone.

Moses was the most meek man in the Bible. Being meek is something you have to practice. Moses was meek, yet the Children of Israel provoked him until he flipped.

We should not allow outside influence to provoke us, in so that we miss the promises of God.

MOSES – THE MEEKEST MAN ON EARTH

Numbers 12:1–3

Despite leading a rebellious nation, Moses did not defend himself when his own siblings, Miriam and Aaron, spoke against him. Instead of retaliating, he left judgment to God. Scripture declares, *"Now the man Moses was very meek, above all the men which were upon the face of the earth."*

DAVID – REFUSING TO KILL SAUL

1 Samuel 24 & 26

Though David had multiple chances to kill King Saul, who was hunting him down to take his life, David restrained himself. He honored Saul as God's anointed and chose the path of humility and patience, leaving vengeance to the Lord.

JOSEPH – FORGIVING HIS BROTHERS

Genesis 45 & 50:15–21

After being betrayed and sold into slavery by his brothers, Joseph rose to power in Egypt. When he had the authority to punish them, he wept and forgave them, saying, *"You meant evil against me, but God meant it for good."*

JESUS CHRIST – THE ULTIMATE EXAMPLE OF MEEKNESS

Matthew 11:29; Isaiah 53:7; Philippians 2:5–8

Jesus described Himself as "meek and lowly in heart." Despite having all power, He submitted to the Father's will, endured suffering silently, and humbled Himself to die on the cross, showing divine meekness in action.

STEPHEN – THE MARTYR WHO PRAYED FOR HIS KILLERS

Acts 7:54–60

As Stephen was being stoned to death for his testimony of Christ, he displayed a Christ-like meekness by praying, *"Lord, lay not this sin to their charge."* His humility and love in the face of violence mirrored Jesus' spirit.

ABRAHAM – LETTING LOT CHOOSE FIRST

Genesis 13:5–11

When strife broke out between Abraham's and Lot's herdsmen, Abraham, though the elder and leader, humbly allowed Lot to choose whichever land he wanted first. He chose peace over power, trusting God to bless him regardless.

JEREMIAH – THE WEEPING PROPHET

Jeremiah 20:7–10; Lamentations 3

Jeremiah endured ridicule, isolation, and persecution for faithfully delivering God's word. Despite his inner pain and sorrow, he meekly submitted to God's calling and never returned evil for evil.

HANNAH – PRAYING WITHOUT RETALIATION

1 Samuel 1:1–20

Though mocked by her husband's other wife, Peninnah, Hannah never lashed out. Instead, she poured out her soul in prayer to God, demonstrating meekness and deep spiritual trust.

RUTH – LOYAL AND HUMBLE SERVANT

Ruth 1–4

Ruth left her homeland to serve Naomi and care for her, saying, "Your people shall be my people, and your God my God." She humbly gleaned in the fields and followed Naomi's instructions, eventually becoming part of the lineage of Christ.

PAUL – ENDURING HARDSHIP WITHOUT COMPLAINT

2 Corinthians 11:23–30; 2 Timothy 4:6–8

Though Paul faced beatings, imprisonment, betrayal, and hardship, he never boasted or became bitter. He viewed his sufferings as opportunities to glorify Christ and modeled meekness in leadership.

SCRIPTURE BACKING:

1. **Numbers 12:3**

   "Now the man Moses was very meek, above all the men which were upon the face of the earth."

2. **Psalm 25:9**

   "The meek will he guide in judgment: and the meek will he teach his way."

3. **Psalm 37:11**

"But the meek shall inherit the earth; and shall delight themselves in the abundance of peace."

4. **Psalm 147:6**

"The Lord lifteth up the meek: he casteth the wicked down to the ground."

5. **Psalm 149:4**

"For the Lord taketh pleasure in his people: he will beautify the meek with salvation."

6. **Isaiah 29:19**

"The meek also shall increase their joy in the Lord, and the poor among men shall rejoice in the Holy One of Israel."

7. **Isaiah 61:1**

"The Spirit of the Lord God is upon me; because the Lord hath anointed me to preach good tidings unto the meek..."

8. **Zephaniah 2:3**

"Seek ye the Lord, all ye meek of the earth, which have wrought his judgment; seek righteousness, seek meekness..."

9. Matthew 5:5

"Blessed are the meek: for they shall inherit the earth."

10. Matthew 11:29

"Take my yoke upon you, and learn of me; for I am meek and lowly in heart: and ye shall find rest unto your souls."

11. Galatians 5:22–23

"But the fruit of the Spirit is love, joy, peace, longsuffering, gentleness, goodness, faith, meekness, temperance…"

12. 1 Peter 3:4

"But let it be the hidden man of the heart, in that which is not corruptible, even the ornament of a meek and quiet spirit…"

T.D. JAKES

(Bishop and Author)

"Gifts can impress people, but fruit is what proves you've been with God. It's the Fruit of the Spirit that gives you staying power."

Chapter Nine

TEMPERANCE (SELF CONTROL)

The Greek word for "temperance" in the Fruit of the Spirit (Galatians 5:22) is εγκράτεια (enkrateia).

Enkrateia means self-control or mastery over one's desires and passions. It refers to:

- The ability to exercise restraint over one's impulses, appetites, and emotions

- A disciplined, controlled life that resists excessive behavior or indulgence

- A fruit of the Spirit that empowers believers to live in alignment with God's will, rather than being controlled by worldly desires

Attending St. George's College, I vividly recall a moment when I had to defend myself in a difficult situation. A classmate who had been bullying others brought a knife to school. In the heat of the moment, I managed to hit the knife out of his hand, and within seconds, he was on the ground. The teacher came in, and when the story was told, I wasn't punished, but the bully faced consequences. Thank God, no one was hurt.

This experience taught me the importance of self-control. Even though I was able to defend myself, I knew who I was, and I didn't let my emotions take over. Your temperament and self-discipline speak volumes about your character. When you maintain self-control, it commands respect from others. It shows that you can be strong when needed, yet still exercise the discipline to handle tough situations peacefully. Your character will always speak for you, especially in moments like these.

It emphasizes inner strength and self-mastery, reflecting the self-discipline that enables a believer to live according to godly principles, even in the face of temptations.

Temperance is a kind of virtue that we have to harness over time. It is having a certain level of self control, even when we are placed to be angry.

He that strives for the mastery is temperate in all things. We cannot allow ourselves to be driven by things. We have to have that level of self control that we overcome fleshly, carnal, mortal urges.

TIPS

1. Spend less than you earn

2. Save before you spend

3. Build an emergency fund

4. Avoid impulse buying

5. Live below your means

6. Track your spending

7. Make a monthly budget

8. Buy quality, not just cheap

9. Avoid emotional spending

10. Focus. on value, not price

JOSEPH – RESISTED POTIPHAR'S WIFE

Genesis 39:7–12

When tempted by Potiphar's wife to commit adultery, Joseph refused repeatedly and fled the situation. His self-control kept him aligned with God's standards, even though it cost him his freedom.

DANIEL – REFUSED THE KING'S FOOD

Daniel 1:8

Daniel purposed in his heart not to defile himself with the king's meat or wine. His disciplined lifestyle and commitment to God's law helped him rise in influence and favor.

DAVID – SPARED SAUL'S LIFE

1 Samuel 24 & 26

Though he had opportunities to kill Saul, who was hunting him, David controlled his emotions and chose to honor Saul as God's anointed. He waited for God's timing rather than taking matters into his own hands.

JESUS – SILENT BEFORE HIS ACCUSERS

Isaiah 53:7; Matthew 27:12–14

Jesus, though falsely accused and mocked, exercised perfect self-control by not defending Himself. He fulfilled prophecy and submitted to the Father's will, trusting in God's justice.

PAUL – DISCIPLINED HIS BODY

1 Corinthians 9:27

"But I keep under my body, and bring it into subjection…" Paul lived a life of spiritual discipline, resisting fleshly impulses to finish his course faithfully and honor Christ.

SCRIPTURE BACKING:

1. **Galatians 5:22–23**

   "But the fruit of the Spirit is love, joy, peace, longsuffering, gentleness, goodness, faith, meekness, temperance: against such there is no law."

2. **Proverbs 25:28**

   "He that hath no rule over his own spirit is like a city that is broken down, and without walls."

3. 1 Corinthians 9:25

"And every man that striveth for the mastery is temperate in all things. Now they do it to obtain a corruptible crown; but we an incorruptible."

4. Titus 1:8

"But a lover of hospitality, a lover of good men, sober, just, holy, temperate;"

(Referring to qualities of a bishop or leader.)

5. Titus 2:2

"That the aged men be sober, grave, temperate, sound in faith, in charity, in patience."

6. 2 Peter 1:5–6

"And beside this, giving all diligence, add to your faith virtue; and to virtue knowledge;

And to knowledge temperance; and to temperance patience; and to patience godliness;"

7. Romans 6:12

"Let not sin therefore reign in your mortal body, that ye should obey it in the lusts thereof."

8. Proverbs 16:32

"He that is slow to anger is better than the mighty; and he that ruleth his spirit than he that taketh a city."

9. 1 Peter 4:7

"But the end of all things is at hand: be ye therefore sober, and watch unto prayer."

10. 2 Timothy 1:7

"For God hath not given us the spirit of fear; but of power, and of love, and of a sound mind."

(A "sound mind" includes discipline and self-control.)

To prevent any form of road rage you may need to apply these gestures and tips to manage road rage and stay calm while driving:

1. **Breathe Deeply:** Take slow, deep breaths to calm your nervous system. Inhale for 4 seconds, hold for 4, exhale for 4.

2. **Count:** BackwardsCounting from 10 to 1 can interrupt your emotional reaction and help you regain focus.

3. **Play Calming Music:** Keep peaceful or uplifting music playing. It can shift your mood and reduce stress.

4. **Leave Early:** Running late increases stress. Give yourself extra time to reach your destination calmly.

5. **Avoid Eye Contact or Gestures:** If another driver is aggressive, don't engage. Avoid looking at them or responding with gestures.

6. **Use Perspective:** Remind yourself: "This isn't personal." The other driver's behavior might be due to their own stress or issues.

7. **Pray or Repeat a Scripture:** Quoting a calming verse (e.g., "He will keep him in perfect peace whose mind is stayed on Him" – Isaiah 26:3) can shift your focus.

8. **Visualize Peace:** Imagine you're surrounded by a bubble of peace. Let negativity bounce off it instead of entering your space.

9. **Avoid Aggressive Driving Habits:** Don't tailgate, speed, or weave through traffic. Driving calmly helps keep your emotions in check.

10. **Pull Over if Needed:** If your anger feels overwhelming, find a safe place to pull over, cool down, and gather your thoughts.

You can use the fruit of the spirit to love your wife as stated below.

1. Love – Selfless, sacrificial care

Love her as Christ loved the Church (Ephesians 5:25). *"I choose to serve and honor her needs above my own."*

2. Joy – Delight in her and in the Lord together

Celebrate her, enjoy her presence, and build a joyful home. *"I will rejoice in our union and bring joy into her life."*

3. Peace – Keep peace in your home and heart

Be the peacemaker, not the agitator (Romans 12:18). *"I create an atmosphere of calm, safety, and harmony."*

4. Longsuffering (Patience) – Be slow to anger and quick to forgive

Endure with grace, even in disagreements or delays. *"I will be patient with her growth and struggles."*

5. **Gentleness – Speak and act with tenderness and care**

Use soft words and loving hands (Colossians 3:19). *"I will never be harsh but always handle her with care."*

6. **Goodness – Do what is morally and spiritually right for her**

Lead with integrity, bless her with kind actions. *"I will do what is best for her, even when no one is watching."*

7. **Faith (Faithfulness) – Be loyal, trustworthy, and consistent**

Keep your word, your vows, and your spiritual covering. *"She can trust me completely because I am committed."*

8. **Meekness – Strength under control**

Lead with humility, not dominance or pride. *"I will lead with love, not lordship."*

9. **Temperance (Self-control) – Discipline in emotions, words, and desires**

Control temper, lust, and selfishness. *"I submit my flesh to the Spirit so I can honor her always."*

Being fruitful individuals came in contact with Jesus and their lives were radically transformed:

1. The Woman with the Issue of Blood - (Mark 5:25–34)

She had been suffering for 12 years, spent all her money on doctors, and was still sick. The moment she touched the hem of Jesus' garment, she was instantly healed. Jesus called her "daughter" and affirmed her faith.

2. The Samaritan Woman at the Well - (John 4:1–30)

A woman with a broken past encountered Jesus at Jacob's well. After speaking with Him, she believed He was the Messiah and became one of the first evangelists, leading many in her town to believe in Christ.

3. Zacchaeus the Tax Collector - (Luke 19:1–10)

He was a wealthy but corrupt man. After meeting Jesus, he repented, gave half his wealth to the poor, and restored fourfold what he had taken. Jesus declared that salvation had come to his house.

4. Mary Magdalene - (Luke 8:2; John 20:11–18)

She had been delivered from seven demons by Jesus. She became a devoted follower and was the first to witness the risen Christ, becoming a key witness to His resurrection.

5. The Demoniac of Gadara - (Mark 5:1–20)

This man was possessed by many demons, lived among tombs, and was uncontrollable. Jesus delivered him, and he became calm, clothed, and in his right mind. He then became a missionary in Decapolis.

6. Blind Bartimaeus - (Mark 10:46–52)

A blind beggar cried out to Jesus for mercy. Jesus healed his blindness, and Bartimaeus followed Him in the way, now with physical and spiritual sight.

7. The Thief on the Cross - (Luke 23:39–43)

One of the criminals crucified with Jesus recognized who He was. Jesus told him, "Today you will be with me in paradise." A deathbed encounter that changed his eternal destiny.

8. Peter the Fisherman - (Luke 5:1–11)

After an encounter with Jesus through a miraculous catch of fish, Peter left everything to follow Him. He became one of the key apostles and foundational leaders in the early Church.

9. The Woman Caught in Adultery - (John 8:1–11)

Instead of condemning her, Jesus offered mercy and told her to "go and sin no more." Her shame was lifted, and her dignity restored.

10. Saul of Tarsus (Apostle Paul) - (Acts 9:1–22)

Although not during Jesus' earthly ministry, the risen Christ encountered Saul on the road to Damascus. A persecutor of Christians became the greatest missionary and writer of much of the New Testament.

11. The Paralyzed Man Lowered Through the Roof - (Mark 2:1–12)

His friends brought him to Jesus through the roof because of the crowd. Jesus first forgave his sins, then healed his body. The man walked out, glorifying God.

12. The Widow of Nain's Son Raised from the Dead - (Luke 7:11–17)

Jesus saw her grieving and had compassion. He raised her only son from the dead, restoring her hope and family.

13. The Ten Lepers - (Luke 17:11–19)

All ten were healed, but one—a Samaritan—returned to give thanks. Jesus not only confirmed his healing but declared him whole, showing that gratitude led to a deeper restoration.

14. Jairus and His Daughter - (Mark 5:21–24, 35–43)

Jairus, a synagogue leader, humbled himself and asked Jesus to heal his dying daughter. Jesus raised her from the dead, proving His power over death.

15. The Roman Centurion - (Matthew 8:5–13)

He showed great faith by asking Jesus to heal his servant from a distance. Jesus marveled at his faith and healed the servant instantly.

16. The Woman Who Was Bent Over for 18 Years - (Luke 13:10–17)

She was physically bowed and could not straighten up. Jesus healed her in the synagogue, releasing her from the spirit of infirmity.

17. The Nobleman's Son - (John 4:46–54)

A royal official pleaded with Jesus to heal his son. Jesus spoke the word, and the boy was healed the same hour. The entire household believed.

18. The Man Born Blind - (John 9:1–41)

Jesus healed him by making mud and sending him to wash in the Pool of Siloam. He was healed both physically and spiritually, and he boldly testified before religious leaders.

19. The Rich Young Ruler (Negative Example) - (Matthew 19:16–22)

He encountered Jesus but walked away sad because he couldn't part with his wealth. This shows that transformation requires surrender.

20. Martha and Mary of Bethany - (Luke 10:38–42; John 11)

Martha learned the value of spiritual devotion. Mary was commended for her worship and sat at Jesus' feet. They both witnessed the resurrection of their brother Lazarus.

21. Lazarus Raised from the Dead - (John 11:1–44)

Four days dead, yet Jesus called him out of the grave. This miracle revealed Jesus as the Resurrection and the Life.

22. The Two Disciples on the Road to Emmaus - (Luke 24:13–35)

They were discouraged after the crucifixion. Jesus walked with them, explained the Scriptures, and revealed Himself in the breaking of bread. Their hearts burned with renewed faith.

CONCLUSION

In the Book of Revelations, the Bible speaks about many fruits, especially in a prophetic or symbolic context, as the Tree of Life mentioned in the Book of Revelation.

Revelation 22:2 (KJV)

"In the midst of the street of it, and on either side of the river, was there the tree of life, which bare twelve manner of fruits, and yielded her fruit every month: and the leaves of the tree were for the healing of the nations."

SYMBOLIC MEANING:

- Tree of Life: Symbolizes eternal life, divine provision, and the presence of God.

- Twelve manner of fruits: Represents fullness, variety, and abundance one for each month, possibly symbolizing continual sustenance and spiritual completeness.

- Leaves for healing: Signifies restoration and wholeness, not just for individuals but for nations.

Psalm 1:1–3 (KJV)

"Blessed is the man that walketh not in the counsel of the ungodly, nor standeth in the way of sinners, nor sitteth in the seat of the scornful.

But his delight is in the law of the Lord; and in his law doth he meditate day and night.

And he shall be like a tree planted by the rivers of water, that bringeth forth his fruit in his season; his leaf also shall not wither; and whatsoever he doeth shall prosper."

SYMBOLISM OF THE TREE IN PSALM 1:

- Planted by rivers of water: The righteous are deeply rooted in the Word of God, constantly nourished.

- Brings forth fruit in season: Their life produces spiritual fruit at the right time, results of obedience, faith, and spiritual maturity.

- Leaf does not wither: Continuous spiritual vitality, even in difficult seasons.

- Whatever they do prospers: God's favor rests upon the righteous.

PSALM 1 CONNECTION TO REVELATION 22:

Both Psalm 1 and Revelation 22 use the image of a fruitful, well-watered tree to represent spiritual life, growth, and blessing. Psalm 1 is about the righteous man on earth. Revelation 22 is about the eternal reward and restoration in God's kingdom.

The tree in Psalm 1 begins the journey of the righteous; the Tree of Life in Revelation 22 completes it in eternal glory.

TREES IN GENESIS:

Tree of Life – Genesis 2:9 (KJV)

"And out of the ground made the Lord God to grow every tree that is pleasant to the sight, and good for food; the tree of life also in the midst of the garden, and the tree of knowledge of good and evil."

- The Tree of Life represents eternal life, divine fellowship, and unbroken access to God's presence.

- After Adam and Eve sinned, access to this tree was cut off (Genesis 3:22–24), symbolizing the loss of eternal life and intimate fellowship with God.

CONNECTING THE THREE TREE THEMES:

1. Genesis – Tree of Life (lost access)

- Located in the Garden of Eden.

- Represents life, blessing, and divine fellowship.

- After sin, mankind is separated from it.

- **Psalm 1 – The Righteous Like a Tree**

- A symbolic restoration through meditating on God's Word.

- Shows what it looks like to live close to God's source of life now: being rooted, fruitful, and spiritually alive.

2. Revelation 22 – Tree of Life (restored access)

- In the New Jerusalem.

- Brings healing, fruit every month, and eternal life.

- Represents restoration of what was lost in Eden through Jesus Christ.

THEOLOGICAL THREAD:

- Genesis: Access lost because of sin.

- Psalm 1: Access modeled through righteous living and delighting in God's Word.

- Revelation: Access restored forever through Christ.

SUMMARY:

The tree in Psalm 1 does relate to the Tree of Life in Genesis and Revelation. It stands as a present-day picture of what it means to live rooted in God, producing fruit, awaiting the full restoration of eternal life in God's Kingdom.

KATHRYN KUHLMAN

(Healing Evangelist)

"The Holy Spirit never leaves behind confusion or disorder, but love, joy, and peace. These are the fruits of His abiding presence."

BENNY HINN

(Healing Minister)

"You can have the anointing, but without the fruit of the Spirit, you will not sustain the anointing. Character keeps you where power puts you."

GETTING ALONG WITH PEOPLE

1. Keep a guard over your words. Speak less than you think, and choose your words wisely.

2. Cultivate a calm and pleasant voice. How you say something often matters more than what you say.

3. Make promises carefully and keep them faithfully, regardless of the cost.

4. Always look for opportunities to speak kindly to or about others. Give praise freely for a job well done, no matter who deserves the credit.

5. Show genuine interest in others their work, their lives, and their families. Let everyone you meet, no matter their status, feel that they matter.

6. Maintain a cheerful attitude. Let your smile speak of hope, even when you're carrying burdens.

7. Keep an open mind in discussions. Disagree if necessary, but avoid arguments. True maturity is shown in the ability to differ respectfully.

8. Let your character speak louder than your words. Refuse to talk about others' faults. Redirect gossip by changing the subject.

9. Be sensitive to the feelings of others. Humor should never come at someone else's expense. Ignore harsh criticism and personal attacks live with such integrity that others won't believe them. Remember: people often criticize others when they're unhappy with themselves.

10. Don't fixate on what you're "owed." Help others simply because it's the right thing to do.

In this book, First Fruits of the Spirit, I recount a memory from my time in Jamaica, where I had two orange trees in the front yard. These trees bore fruit abundantly. However, there were times when some branches became dry and unproductive. To encourage healthy growth and more fruitful yield, we had to prune these dry branches.

This practice of pruning is symbolic of spiritual growth. Just as fruit trees are meant to bear fruit, our spiritual lives are designed to bear the fruits of the Spirit. When we encounter spiritual dryness, it is essential to remove obstacles and seek renewal, allowing us to flourish and produce abundant spiritual fruit.

REFERENCES CITED

1. The Matthew Henry Commentary

2. The Holman Bible Dictionary

3. The Strong's, Concordance

4. KJV Bible

5. Wv Grant Faith Books

6. Greek Dictionary Google

7. Bing

James 3:18 The Fruit of righteousness is sown in peace of them that make peace.

James 5:7 Be patient therefore, brethren, unto the coming of the Lord. Behold, the husbandman waiteth for the precious fruit of the earth, and hath long patience for it, until he receive the early and latter rain.

In a world where the gifts of the Holy Spirit are highly sought after, it's essential to remember that being anointed and using these gifts is meant for the Kingdom. However, in our personal and spiritual lives, the fruit of the Spirit plays a vital role. It uplifts and builds up the body of Christ, aligning our spirit with character and integrity. Even if you possess spiritual gifts, without character, it can damage your reputation. But when the fruit of the Spirit is present, it builds your character and integrity, allowing the gifts of the Spirit to flow freely and operate in the right sequence. Integrity is foundational in the body of Christ. As my former pastor would say, 'You do not want to deface the name of Jesus Christ with your level of self and mortality. Instead, crucify your flesh, operate in the Spirit, and build up the name of Jesus Christ.' This book, essentially, is for the edification and clarification with the fruit of the Spirit."